Songs of African Fathers

(The flavour of African Poetry)

By

Mniko Chacha

Contacts: Send me an email to

mnikochacha@yahoo.co.uk

<u>Dedication:</u>

I humbly dedicate this book to my lovely daughter, Loyce.

## Table of Contents.

# PART I.

Poem: Africa and Ignorance.

Perhaps, Africa and ignorance,
Are enemies and best friends at once,

Many times, Africa acts in ignorance,
Its citizens get hurt in tolerance,

Maybe, Africa has a lifelong love affair with ignorance,

Because I don't see a serious severance,

Since then, my Africa fell asleep,
A sleepyhead land, who will wake it up?

Some Africans are far to the limit of ignorance,
Should they say no or be submissive to ignorance?

From hence,
Ignorance is a big fence,

As a consequence,
Africa's intellect is dying in silence,

At a glance,
Africans must unite to cease ignorance,

It makes sense,
To end its existence,

African schools must fight ignorance,
By teaching worth education and self-reliance,

Maybe, one day African schools will strength
brains,

But many of them don't have books and libraries!

Ten to ten,
Ignorance beats Africa with a cane,

Ignorance is a pain in the neck,
Africa should get it in the neck,

Maybe, one day Africa will learn to earn,
Knowledge and shine,

Once Africa gets the pill of ignorance, will lead a
change,
And be the change,


Poem: The Missing Rib.


The missing rib is my future woman,

That will be my right woman,

My endless love,

She will fit me like a glove.

Please show me the appropriate woman,

The distinguishable woman,

The grown-up woman,

That will be my number one.


I am aged and old,

Still, I am not married,

Just show me one decent woman,

That I will marry and win.


I won't fear her bare feet,

I will love her at first sight,

She will be my first and last,

She will replace the missing rib in my chest.


Show me a woman with valour,

The lady who appreciates her skin colour,

And understands her position in the society,
A woman who doesn't like enmity.


I won't fear her faults,
I will accept her flaws,
Please show me only one woman,
That I can marry and win.


She must behave like a dove,
And be a great friend of love,
And an enemy of hate,
I will know her once we meet.


Show me the obedient one,
I will adore her and be the only one,
For her life,
And make her my wife.

Don't show me the work-shy woman,

Show me the active woman,

The superior in quality,

That will assist me on ending poverty.


Show me the humble and smart woman,

It is not easy to know the one,

But the right one is somewhere else,

I will marry her and be on the rise.


Show me a woman with mutual trust,

A woman whom I will trust,

At last.

She will end my longing thirsty.

Show me the woman,

That will be a good mother to my children,

If you show me the right one,

I will get married all of a sudden.


Poem: Fat Crocodiles.


I lived nearby rivers,

The rivers were homes to skinny reptiles,

Those animals had long jaws,

Long tails,

Short legs,

Human faces,

And unsatisfied mouths.

By that time, they preached love,

And purported to show love,

They were polite like a dove,

Their speeches attracted like the gravity,

Erroneously, we believed their sincerity,

Because all of them had gone to schools,

But they're educated ones with deceitful minds.


Still, I remember yesteryears,

When all of them had human faces,

Ascetic mouths,

Disciplined ears,

And decent personalities,

They spoke gently and civilized,

Basing on those traits, we were deceived.


They looked so skinny,

And scrawny,

So, they begged us for food,

For the sake of building the brotherhood,

We accepted to give them food,

In return, they confirmed,

To protect us when we could cross the rivers

To look for more food.


They ate our food and became corpulent,

And breached the agreement,

By drowning us into the sea,

I blamed and said. "Let me see.

Why do they deceive us?

Why do they trap us?

Why do they double–cross us?"


Our farms were beyond the rivers,

They restrained us to cross rivers,

To collect food for our families.

We were quite a few crew,

But they ceased our life every few,

We cried for help,

But they didn't give us a leg up,


We tried again to cross the rivers,

To take food for our empty stomachs,

But their excellency crocodiles,

Forbade all of us,

We roared. "Fighting for our welfare is beneficent,

And munificent."

We fought fire with fire and made them non-
existent.


Poem: The circumcision.

I got a red invitation card,
To attend the circumcision ceremony,

Where women lost their clitoris in painful way.

I attended with a sympathy card,

I thought. "What could happen there,

If I could not be able to endure,

Watching a woman screaming,

For loosing important part of her body?"

A secret organ of her body.


Then, I decided to take care,

Before I took steps towards the residence,

Where the circumciser did her ugly assignment,

She had a brave face, that old woman.

One of her assistants brought her a razor,

A sharpen razor designed by the ancestors,

So as to cut the genital body organs,

of teen girls.


All girls sat on black traditional chairs,

Uncomfortably with sadly faces.

It was a command for every girl,

To obey and seat in total nakedness.


Then, a watchman told me to open my eyes,

So as to witness the cruelty celebration,

And see how a dark razor cut away,

The significant organ of a girl's body.


"Ooooooohhh, don't kill me the circumciser."

One girl screamed and shouted.

I felt her pain,

But the circumciser smiled,

And said. "Endure to be a perfect woman."

The girl bled hopelessly,

There was no way,

The soil ancestors drank,

Her innocent blood.


Poem: My AFRICA.


My Africa,

Do you remember your old days?

Those painful historical days,

When you fought slavery,

And won the little victory,


You won the fight,

And initiated the light,

But the same light is fading,

From the hill of freedom, you are falling,

And worrying,

I watch breaking news.

And see your hopeless graduates,

Dying in drowning after a hit by cruel sea waves,

When they sail to escape your doors,

Through the Mediterranean Sea to overseas,

They escape to find jobs in abroad,

Like washing one's legs,

Or one's lips!

And be paid few dollars.

My Africa stop being a toad,

You are rich by resources,

Still, you have nothing in hands,

Except poor health infrastructures,

And population of jobless graduates,

The great thing you have is greedy leaders!

You own minerals you can't sell,

You must know why you fails,

Your neighbors have kin leaders,

But you keep thieves in state houses,

'The day robbers of your resources.'


You have tried to have elites,

And got engineers you can't trust,

Those neighbors build your state houses,

Then, you say you have engineers!

Some of your doctors can't even heal patients,


You are abandoning your identity,

And quality,

I know you were deceived with insincerity,

That every culture of you is bad,

Oppressive, barbaric and outdated,


I have a word for you,

To become the best of you,

Please change first your mindset,

Emerge the new light,

Be the bright.


Poem: Songs of African Fathers.


Mwalimu Julius K. Nyerere sang

from Tanzania,

Dr. Kwame Nkrumah sang

from Ghana,

And Nelson Mandela chorused

from South Africa,

All of them sang,

The liberation song titled 'We can.'

They wanted Africa to become one,

At least they won.


Hon. Jomo Kenyatta sang

from Kenya,

Hon. Kenneth Kaunda sang

from Zambia,

And John Okero sang

from Uganda,

They stood togcther and sang,

The same song named. 'We can.'

They said Africa is for Africans,

At least they won.


They sang for education,

And poverty eradication,

They fought for ignorance's elimination,

They became one for Africa's unification,

They did all with caution,

Because it cost blood for liberation,

They said. "We must win this mission."


Sir Seretse khama from Botswana

sang with passion,

He said. "A nation without a past is not a nation."

He united Botswana as one nation,

And won to sing the song of liberation,

He sang it with a clear mission,

And fought the battle by action,

Finally, he made his country a peaceful nation.


Martin Luther King Jr. sang,

From abroad with a good intention,

He sang the same song of liberation,

'African liberation,'

He wanted Africans to be recognized as God's creation.

He did all with caution,

Because it cost blood for liberation.


Samora Machel sang

from Mozambique,

He sang the same song named. 'We can.'

And said. "Of all things we have done,

the most important-the one,

that history will record as principal contribution,

of our generation,

is that we will understand how to turn,

the armed struggle

into revolution.''


Julius K. Nyerere sang for liberation,

He sang in Arusha declaration,

To boost social-economy as a nation,

He fought ignorance to build acknowledgeable
nation,

And hate tribalism for unification,

At least he won,

And led Tanzania to a great unification.

Call them friends of amalgamation,

And integration,

Because all of them loved the liberation,

They suffered for their states unification,

All of them had a great vision,

They brought all Africans in unification,

At least they won.


Hastings Kamuzu Banda from Malawi

had a word for us.

He said. "There is a future in Africa for all of us,

for the majority and minority races and tribes."

He worked for Africans,

He saw a future in Africa despite of tribal differences.

He was one of the African lions.

That insisted Africans to have the future plus.


Hon. Samora Machel from Mozambique,

Fought against colonialism,

Exploitation and injustice,

He believed that all races in the world

want liberty and independence.

He said. "There is no place for white racism,

as there is no place for black racism,

because racism in its essence is an organized

attitude, reactionary attitude."

Julius K. Nyerere from Tanzania

Sow the seeds of education,

His people called him. 'Father of the Nation,'

He said. "Education is not a way to escape poverty,

it is a way of fighting it."

He begged all Africans to unite,

And insisted them to fight poverty,

With sincerity,


Julius K. Nyerere taught the emancipation,

To his people for the African liberation,

He spoke. "No nation,

has the right to make decisions

for another nation;

people for another people."

And fought for sovereignty of his nation,

He reminded his people,

"Development comes through cooperation."


Julius K. Nyerere gave Africa

an encouragement,

He rooted his leadership

on people's development,

He said. "You cannot develop people,

you must allow people

to develop themselves."

And taught his people to work for themselves,

But he reminded his fellow africans,

"Without unity, there is no future for Africa."


Julius K. Nyerere sang for stability and change,

He dreamed to see Africa in a comfort angle,

He spoke. "If a door is shut,

attempts should be made to open it,

if it is a jar; it should be pushed,

until it is wide open,

in neither case the door should

be blown up at the expense of those inside."


The African father kept on singing,

For the development of Africans.

He said. "If real development is to take place,

the people have to be involved."

My writing pen sings the same song,

If we want Africa to be developed,

Our leaders should first allow people to be

developed.


The same African father cautioned,

That all Africans shall hate tribalism,

And foster africanism.

He said. "In Tanzania it was more than

one hundred tribal units

which lost their freedom,

it was one nation that regained it."

He built his nation without tribalism,

But with strong unity.

Hon. Jomo Kenyatta from Kenya

taught Africans to work hard,

He said. "Many people may think that,

now I can see the sun of freedom shinning,

richness will pour down

like manna from heaven,

I tell you there will be nothing from heaven,

We must all work hard with our hands,

to save ourselves from poverty,

ignorance and disease."


The same father from Kenya

sang again for prosperity,

He believed that our land

is African property.

He said. "God said this is our land,

land in which we flourish as people,

we want our cattle to get fat on our land,

so that our children grow up in prosperity,

and we don't want the fat be removed to feed

others."


He sang again about African children,

And called people to be role models

of African children.

He said. "Our children may learn about

the heroes of the past,

our task is to make ourselves,

the architects of the future."

And insisted to shape the future for our children,

The future Africa will be led by nowadays children.


The same African father sang again

for cultural identity,

And African identity,

He loved African culture,

He said. "Africans were left in peace

on their own lands,

Europeans would have to offer

the benefits of white civilization,

. . . they would have to left Africans choose

what parts of European culture,

could be beneficially transplanted

 and how they could be adapted."


Samora Machel from Mozambique

sang for good leadership.

He said. "The state must be the first to be organized

and totally committed,

to serving the interests of the people."

And gave a unique mentorship,

That African leaders should hate selfishness,

And be hardly committed,

To work for African people.


Again, and again,

He sang for African unity.

He said. "Unity and victory are synonymous."

And told the reality,

If all African people unite,

Africa will win the fight,

Against ignorance, poverty,

Tribalism, corruption and leader's insincerity.


Samora Machel echoed again

about solidarity,

He preached strongly

about African solidarity.

He said. "Solidarity is not an act of charity,

but mutual aid,

between forces fighting for the same objective."

His words are productive,

Solidarity should be the African motive.


Dr. Kwame Nkrumah of Ghana

sang for African liberation,

And stood firm for African emancipation.

He said. "The independence of Ghana

is meaningless,

unless it is linked-up,

with the total liberation

of the African continent."

He worked for Africa's liberation,

And became the hero of emancipation.

Kwame Nkrumah sang again

for awareness,

And spoke. "We have awakened,

will not sleep anymore today,

from now on,

There is a new Africa in the world."

Africans awareness must grow on,

Awareness should be the first lesson,

To teach any African child.


The Ghanaian father sang again for freedom,

In his words I see wisdom,

He said. "Freedom is not something,

that one people can bestow

on another as a gift,

they claim it as their own,

and none can keep it from them."

Then, Africa to be free from

any kind of slavery is a must,

but not a gift.


This father whispered

for sovereignty,

That sovereignty should bring African prosperity.

He said. "No people without a government

of their own can expect to be treated

on the same level,

as people of independent sovereign states,

it is better to be free to govern

or misgovern yourself,

than to be governed by anybody else. . . ."


Dr. Kwame Nkrumah chorused the African unity,

He believed on it,

And said. "We must find an African solution,

and thus this can only

be found in African unity,

divided we are weak,

united, Africa could become

one of the great forces

for good in the world."

Nelson Mandela, anti-apartheid icon,

The real African son,

Sang to all leaders in African land.

He said. "Real leaders must be ready

to sacrifice all for the freedom of their people."

African leaders should hate selfishness

And lead by improving real freedom to their

people.


The same African father warbled

for education,

'A tool for African liberation,'

He spoke. "Education is the most powerful

weapon,

which you can use to change the world.''

This is the truth and revelation,

'Education for liberation,'

Because it's a machine for emancipation.


He quavered for freedom,

With words of wisdom.

He said. "To be free is not merely

to cast off one's chains

but to live in a way that respects,

and enhances freedom of others."

So, Africans should live by respecting each other,

And one another,

Tata Madiba sang for determination,

'Something that brings victory.'

He spoke. "When people are determined,

They can overcome anything."

My Africa today lacks determination,

It loose slowly its liberation.

It better unites with strong determination.


King Haile Sellasie sang from Ethiopia,

For knowledge,

'A fuel to travel a mileage.'

He said. "Knowledge is power,

if it is not applied proper to create,

let there be no doubts, it will destroy."

Africans should hunt knowledge

To create goodness in Africa.


This Ethiopian man sang

For good leadership,

He said. "A good leader maintains a balance,

between emotional drive,

and sound thinking."

Good leaders will keep Africa moving,

But evil leaders will keep Africa sinking,

With good leaders Africa will be shinning.


Poem: Africa on tomorrow.


I look my Africa on the mirror,

To forecast its tomorrow,

Will it be a land of sorrow?

Or a land of milk flow?


Poverty is our historical error,

Ignorance is our bed pillow,

Africans try but it restrained us to grow,

And initiate the beginning of our sorrow.


I still look on the mirror,

Will Africa rise or fall?

Without binding to its good moral,

I think it will soar sore and blow.


Then, I look again on the mirror,

And see little things we like to borrow,

Puppet leaders lead against the rule of law,

Steal our minerals, wealth and own all.


Before long, I see one corrupt leader,

That does not fear ignorance

And poverty at all,

But he fears the word 'overthrow,'

Overthrowing him is something we vow.


Thus, I learn from the mirror,

That our Africa must glow,

And our reasoning grow,

To stand upright and go,

Then, our children will follow.

If Africa want to beat someone hollow,

It must stand tall,

And quit from borrowing little things and more,

To create its independent life and escape this
sorrow.


Finally, I see on the mirror,

The next Africa will be the lowest of the low,

And unstable because it allows rebels to grow.

Africa will be the fighting mall.


Poem: The Hungry Voters.


Here is a story of the skinny voters,

Others call them 'the hungry voters,'
If you wish call them 'The greedy voters.'


They gave up their life with few dollars,
And chose (a leader) an agent of failures,
Only because he gave them dollars,


They got angry when I named them,

'Friends of bribe dealers,'
And 'the sellers of votes.'


Before long, they learned from their own mistakes,
And aggrieved by their empty stomachs,
All of them began to call him a spade,

He took their monies,

And bought for himself luxury cars,

He drove criminally the new cars,

And hit them in the streets,



He was kin in attending all clubbing events,

But not rational public events,

He didn't solve people's problems,

And never responded to calamities,



His busy selfishness,

And heedlessness,

Made things go astray,

Still, he persecuted them to obey.



One day, he uttered on television screen,

"Our economy is rapidly growing

from zero to hero."

"We don't care, we are hungry," the hungry voters

replied.

And marched aggressively across the streets.


They quoted one Philosopher who wrote

in his non existing book that,

"Some leaders are poor in ethics.

They are very serious patients,

And fake Painters that change the white truth

to be seen as dark lies."


(Hungry voters,)

Ran to the tallest hill,

And raised their voice again and again,

"An empty stomach never stops

to ask for food."

They chorused again with pain,

"An empty stomach,

never cease to fight for food."

Then, they left to homes.


Time ahead,

He announced the state emergency,

And got surprised,

About how the hungry voters united against him,


He drove a bullet proof car to the tallest hill,

So as to talk with his hungry voters,

All of them asked him about unfulfilled promises,

And improper use of public funds,

He replied.

"I think I will buy gold comets for all of you

so that everyone of you will be rich."

They shouted endlessly.

And said. "We are not hungry of gold comets

but we are hungry of justice."


They still marched forward and protested,

Until when their leader resigned,

Hopelessly and left the throne,

They won.


## PART II.

Poem: A tale of Tax Collector.


The taxes I paid responsibly,

Paved no any way for development,

The tax collector insisted me to pay with courage,

Yes, I paid with courage,


Then, I thought a little bit and said,

"Maybe, tomorrow will be a good day,

Street roads will be constructed and

health services be improved."
Still today, nothing is improved,


The taxes I pay with humanity,

I pay to develop my street,

And not otherwise,

But the tax collector uses my taxes

For his own pleasure,


He deceives me to pay more tax,

For my street development.

He doesn't care how I pay tax with hunger,

He is more than a grief.


I pay more tax with an empty stomach,

To build my street,

Tax paying is no longer a profit,

But loss to my street,


It is no longer a citizen duty but a burden.

I am commanded to pay it unconditionally,

I am silenced not to ask the use of my tax money,

Even when things go astray.


My neighbors and I never get a break,

From the tax collector's noise,

Through day and night,

He insists us to pay tax without questioning.


No social services are available in my street,

There is no efficient electricity,

There is no clean and safe water,

But he is buying luxury cars with my tax,


He spends my tax throughout a year,

When we ask him, he roars to us,

"No body of you is allowed to ask me because

It is a sin to challenge the almighty tax collector."


We live in a sealed bottle,

Where our voices can't be heard.


The tax collector is my neighbour,

He uses my tax unnecessarily to travel abroad,


He pays the school fees for his royal kid,

And billed him a balanced diet in abroad,

He thinks that it is holy to steal fruits of my labour,

"The less considered labour."

I am paying him more taxes,

For his personal interests,

My children are expelled from schools,

Because I pay taxes and fail to pay school fees,


He is a role model to his greedy child.

And other royal children from tax collectors'
families,

All of them dream to study hard,

And later be employed as 'Thieves-Tax collectors.'


They dream to strengthen their financial

empires.

By stealing our taxes,

Still, they call themselves 'The blessed

And anointed.'


But, the other side of my brain,

Insists me to reason and make a decision,

Either to pay tax with an empty stomach,

Or to quit the game and feed my stomach.


Poem: Please Wait.


At the reception yard,
Many patients stood by the yard,
The watchman stood up and said.
"Have a seat," meanwhile, he insisted,

"Sit down,

And never make a conversation."


In a twinkling, I stood up to knock the door,

So as to beg the doctor to save my soul,

But the watchman gave me a low blow,

And injured my ill jaw,


Abruptly, the Doctor came out,

And said.

"Please wait, you must wait."

Then, he left us abandoned,


Then, I telephoned him after the long wait,

"Please wait."

The doctor said on phone without respect,

And asked for a bribe to give me hospitality,

Hence, I asked a passer-by,
"Why hospitals become the bribe houses?"
She answered.
"Some doctors study only medicine without
hospitality."


Poem: Live like A Stick Insect.


One day I made a thorough learning,
And wondered how a stick insect makes a living.


It is a smart brained insect ever being,
That never tired of waking up early the morning.


It is well organized and focused in joint working,
And never works for today only but for the future
living.

It is the food collector for a future living,
And a very brilliant insect in food keeping.

Please study its living,
And makes your future shinning.

A stick insect never afraid of falling,
Because it keeps standing up and forward moving.

When its life is souring,
It applies techniques of life sobering.

It acts dead to escape the imminent killing,
Once an enemy left, it keeps on moving.

Learn to a stick insect, get skills of living,
Never afraid failures but keep on moving.

When an enemy initiate your killing,

Sometimes, acts a dead while living.

Imitate the stick insect's living,
For your success and life longing.

Poem: Fifty fifty movement.

I heard a female cry from the midst of men,

Unnumbered men stood up,

From the dust of my father's land Africa,

And protested the female cry,

Some men opposed with cruel voices,

While others protested to protect their traditions.

They said. "We must protect taboos and honour

our ancestors."

After a while, a female cry increased twice,

But many men called it unwise,


They thought it intended to steal their authority,

Or it intended to disrupt their traditional power as
men.

Other men thought that the female cry was a threat,


They shouted again and again,

"African marriages are going to hell,

if we can't prevent women

from overcoming us."


Women cried and shed tears,

For ownership rights, educational rights,

And social rights,


A least their cry got attention of some men.

Few men accepted their initiative as a positive one,

But many men called it "Indiscipline movement."


Women cried for their security and protection,

Girls echoed their voice against early

And forced marriage,

All of them stood against rape from unwise men,


Their cry touched the atmosphere of justice,

Some men understood the intended message,

But many men protested against everything,

Another woman cried for being circumcised by force,

After she was arrested to attend the circumcision palace,

By her old brothers who wanted her to be a perfect woman through circumcision.


Women wanted to be recognized as equal to men,

And be free from unwise men,

They wanted to own and inherit property,


They called some taboos 'barbaric,'

And aimed for the battle with men.

Some men called them 'The enemies of ancestors.'

Some families broke,

And many marriages fell,

Because women wanted to be equal to men!

Poem: The Son of a Watchman.

Since I met him, it is twenty years ago,
The street called him 'a night watchman,'
He was blessed with one begotten son.

He loved his son,
And took care of him,
He worked hard for him.

He believed that love is above all,

And found faith on love,

He known the power of love.

He preached love at home,

And taught love by wise words,

He shown love by actions,

All of his actions engineered love.

He adored love,

And said. "Love brings success."

He guarded walls without worries.

Through the darkest night times,

But it was not an easy job for him,

He worked with love.

And took his begotten son to school,

The son schooled to the university level.

He taught his son to love himself,

And berg him to love others,

He insisted him to learn forgiving others,


The watchman put love first,

His spirit lifted up many men,

All men loved to hear his wise words.


He said to him. "If love is found at home,

At the work place or anywhere else,

Then, success should be there."


Later, his son graduated with success,

He didn't forget to remind him to love others.

He said. "Blessings come from others."


After the passing of many years,

The watchman became an old boy,

And quitted his job,

He found a rest at home.

Few days later,

His son was employed,

Before long, the watchman passed away,

And left his family in paranoid.

Endlessly, they mourned.

His son became the boss,

And refused to love others,

Love was nothing to him.

He became a successful man,

And demeaned to love,

As a consequence, he married lusts.

He abandoned his lovely woman,

And began a love affair with a strange woman,

Soon, he chased away his JULIANA,

JULIANA was his decent woman,
But he abandoned her,
For the useless strange woman,

He grabbed her from the corners of alcoholic bars,
Where she was selling her body to many men,
Men called her 'For all.'

JULIANA remained the decent woman,
And the ex-wife of the watchman's son,
The woman who was created for him,

The son of a watchman,
Left JULIANA in a lonely desert,
So, she mourned and worried,

From that moment,

He began drinking alcohol in bars with
his new woman until he became famous
And untouchable,

JULIANA begged him,
And said to him.
"Never forget love for lusts."

The beautiful words of JULIANA,
Never changed his adultery heart,
He was busy with the new woman,

He called JULIANA 'the barbaric woman,
And outdated woman.'
He abandoned her in shame.

Few days later,
The strange woman launched his journey of
sorrow,

She failed him,

She gave a blank cheque to him,
A cheque that turned back marked,
"No sufficient love."

At the same time,
She married another man,
And abandoned him,

He was grieved,
And memorised the words of his late father,
"Never marry lusts at all."

He jumped into the love pond,
And failed to swim across,
He was stuck like a drowning toad,

The strange woman said.

"Money is the only shield,
in love field."

He was left in a breakup cold,
And stubbed,
By the strange woman.

He looked too weird,
He said.
"Women are wicked."

Then, he shouted.
"I am betrayed by my bed friend,
I am finished."

He created his own bad luck,
His life became so sad,
She gave him a letter marked "Women Are
Wicked."

Day after day, he lost the working standards,
Soon thereafter, he was fired,
And became jobless,

It was a painful life episode,
Because he was depressed,
And worried,

He began stealing,
To make a living,
And thriving,

One day, he was arrested,
And remanded,
His freedom ceased,

Soon, he was taken to the court of law,
And found guilty,

Hence, the hearing session ended,

The Judge read the judgment,
Convicted him,
And sentenced him,

He was jailed,
Confined,
And punished,

Fifteen years later,
He was released,
And freed,

Love never become old,
He remarried JULIANA,
His right woman,

Always, JULIANA was his best friend,

And his best candy,

With JULIANA, he got the best end,


## PART III.

Poem: Two men with one hoe.


Two men were friends,

They had a great mission,

To make their home land,

A better land for food provision.


Those men were determined,

To accomplish their mission,

They loved their home land,

To the extent of winning their mission.


Then, they decided to buy one hoe,

So as to make a better cultivation,

They hold on courageously,

To clear the forest.

Soon after clearing the land,

They debated,

About who could use the hoe?

They fought each other and forget their mission.

They fought for one hoe,

To build their nation,

And called each other 'bad names.'

That was the death of their mission.

They failed to use one hoe,

To foster their cultivation,

Instead, they brought chaos on their land,

Many souls died during their confrontation.

They were all leaders,

All of them were blessed with a hoe for unification,

But their selfishness killed the goal,

The goal of building one nation.


Poem: My Hungry Teeth.

My teeth,

Obey me,

Be the humble guards of my mouth,



My teeth,

Listen to me,

Don't be rude once you see my neighbour's food,



My hungry teeth,

Give all ears to me,

Don't look at me, I have nothing to put in food pots,


My friendly teeth,

Have mercy on me,

Endure a day without opening the empty pots,


My teeth,

Keep quiet,

But keep on dreaming for a balanced diet,


Don't chew nothing to make noises,

Keep calm under the lips,

Getting a balanced diet is like herding cats,

It takes a time,

Just give me more time,

Tomorrow will be fine,

Few people encourage you,

But many demean you,

I am here to comfort you,

Take hungry as a lesson,

Move on, just go on,

I will fed you well on tomorrow,

You know that my poor dad,

Took me to school,

And insisted me to study hard,



You know how I did it all,

But schooling only doesn't bring food at all,

I am thinking a way to break the jobless wall.



Maybe, a white-collar job is not for me,

But times never be the same,

I will fight until I get out of this shame,

Success needs commitment and long wait,

I will work and wait,

Until I make it,


Sorry my hungry teeth,

I know that you are sick,

But no hospital can cure you without insurance,


There is no doctor who can smile at you,

Without giving him a reason to smile,

Money is that reason,


Only the heaven stands with you,

But the world is against you,

I am the only helper around you,



It is painted on a restaurant's door,

"No money, no food,

You get what you can afford."



This is a capitalist world,

You are hungry because I can't buy you food,

I get only what I can afford,



Have courage,

To travel a mileage,

Things will change,

Give me a breath,

Keep calm into my mouth,

One day I will be wealth,

My own teeth,

Understands me,

Because one day I will bring food on the table,

Poem: A slave.

I am a bond-slave,

I am handcuffed, I can't even wave,

My mentor taught me to behave,

Even when the slavery is grave,

He begged me to be submissive like a dove,

Otherwise, the slave master will bury me in a

grave,


Being a slave is a life-and-death decision,

Many slavers work to develop the mission,

Of their slave masters,

That pretend to act like holy bosses,

Still, slavery is the destruction of humanity,

And dignity,


Slavery breach the standards of humanity,

Magnanimity,

Generosity,

Sympathy and pity,

It is inhumanity,

And cruelty.


Poem: The fall of X empire.


The king can't believe,
That he must leave,
From the crown because his people want him to
leave,
And give power to another brave,


He doesn't behave,
He is the military offensive,
He burns his people with a stove,
And consign them to the grave.

He calls himself 'the life president,'

Whoever challenges him is called 'the imprudent,'

He lookalike,

'The master thief of the national cake,'


He acts childish to gain fame,

His people are tired of him,

They want to drag him,

They call him 'a shame,'


There is no one he can blame,

Because he designed his own shame,

By killing the national dream,

And stealing the state cream,


He says. "I can't step down,

I have armies to protect my crown from being

overthrown."

But one of his voters replies,

"The power of people is bigger than your armies."

They hold on pushing down his crown,

Until the surrender of his army,

His empire is worn,

And the king is overthrown.


THANK YOU FOR READING.


MY SECOND BOOK AND OTHER BOOKS ARE AVAILABLE ON AMAZON WEBSITE, KOBO WEBSITE, AND SMARSHWORD WEBSITE WITH ITS DISTRIBUTION WEBSITES. GRAB YOUR COPY, ENJOY THE READ.